WE WANT

COMICS BY JASHORN

Marshall Cavendish
Editions

Published by Marshall Cavendish Editions
An imprint of Marshall Cavendish International

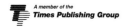

A member of the
Times Publishing Group

Other Marshall Cavendish Offices:
Marshall Cavendish Corporation, 800 Westchester Ave, Suite N-641, Rye Brook, NY 10573, USA • Marshall Cavendish International (Thailand) Co Ltd, 253 Asoke, 16th Floor, Sukhumvit 21 Road, Klongtoey Nua, Wattana, Bangkok 10110, Thailand • Marshall Cavendish (Malaysia) Sdn Bhd, Times Subang, Lot 46, Subang Hi-Tech Industrial Park, Batu Tiga, 40000 Shah Alam, Selangor Darul Ehsan, Malaysia

Marshall Cavendish is a registered trademark of Times Publishing Limited

National Library Board, Singapore Cataloguing in Publication Data

Name(s): Jashorn.
Title: We want comics / by Jashorn.
Description: Singapore : Marshall Cavendish Editions, [2023]
Identifier(s): ISBN 978-981-5066-93-7 (paperback)
Subject(s): LCSH: Caricatures and cartoons. | Singaporean wit and humor, Pictorial.
Classification: DDC 741.5695957--dc23

Printed in Singapore

For my Mom & Dad. ♥♥

FOREWORD

I've been drawing since cartoons were a fixture on Saturday mornings. As a six-year old, my parents were surprised that I was copying Transformer robots from the TV with a pencil instead of watching with an open jaw at proceedings as most did. They tried bringing me to drawing competitions but these were a big failure as all this attention-fickle kid did was stare at Star Wars action figures at the next door toy store window.

It wasn't till high school that I found my stride in art class. Practice warnings from a stern teacher meant my right hand finally got the practice it needed from weekly classes. Again, my attention strayed again toward Marvel comics and a series of comics that grabbed my heart and made my cheeks constantly smirk. Both *Bizarro and The Far Side* comics had such a huge impact on my insides (heart, ribs and all) that I didn't realize a college degree in psychology and a short stint in marketing communications couldn't keep the child in me from trying my hand at doing the same thing Mr Larson did years after my adult career.

A simple dare from one of my church friends was all it took.

What started as fan art on Instagram soon evolved into work after work of my own as I came up with jokes like a gambling machine on steroids. Next thing I knew I was drawing single panel comics like a swimmer who went for daily Olympics training.

Thankfully, I loved it. After half a decade of enjoyable drawing, I was asked if a compilation of comics in a book was in order. I jumped at the opportunity.

Gladly I now present to you, my first half decade of comics. Have fun. :D

Rex soon realized it wasn't the Main Door of the House he should watch constantly.

It can be a Horrid time for Werewolves when it's only a Partial Full Moon.

Romantic times of Modern Domestic Mice.

The secret luxurious life of Designer Boutique Dust Mites in New York.

"Hate to point out the obvious, Sir.
Seems we're in the middle of Nowhere."

Having a dog named Shark was
often disastrous at the Beach.

Overweight Mountain Goats shouldn't take Scenery Photos.

It made perfect sense. We kidnap her, we'd get all the Chicks in the park.

After hitting on her, Igor finally found himself a new Wife.

Watch out – Huge Fans EVERYWHERE!!!

It's pretty wild what Climate Change
can do to your Local Habitat.

Pillow Abuse Anonymous

Making Mountains out of Molehills.

Things got unnervingly weird
when Robert returned from
the Dentist with new Dentures.

Even the Tooth Fairy got greedy sometimes.

"Sorry Sir, in order for this to work you badly need to stop playing the Field."

Until the Virus Home Quarantine I never understood why my Dog was always begging me to go outside.

Sometimes we Mums just need a 5-minute Break.

It takes an entire Nest to please the whims
and fantasies of one Royal Gal.

Many who hit the Bottle early are
the hardest to please.

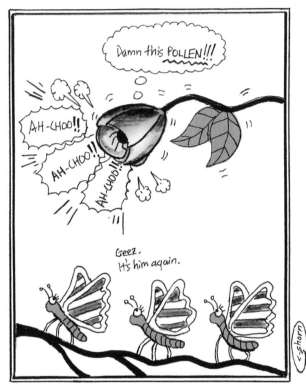

It was too obvious for Helen and her
girlfriends where the Spider-Ambush was.

"Of course it's inaccessible bro. They don't call this place Hell for nothing you know."

With a single Leap, Moby beat all his Competitors and set a new World Record.

It isn't always Healthy having
the Hospital Morning Radio on.

Stand-up Comedy at Snake Bars can be
Murderous. Nobody claps, everyone hisses.

"It's the Laundry, Doc. It scares me."

Rex never faltered in his duty to protect everyone from those Window Monsters.

"You may have fallen for her, Dominic, but (ouch)
it seems she WANTS to keep her distance from ya!"

It's hard running away from Dentally Healthy Sharks.

In a cruel but inspired move, Todd and Dan put the empty Tomato Sauce bottles they found to good use.

Jonathan suddenly remembers leaving the Toilet Paper upstairs before rushing down.

A germaphobe, the new Pope couldn't cope without using Antiseptic Soap.

Needless to say, Rapunzel hated having a younger brother who loved Swings.

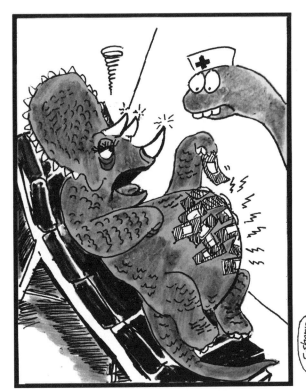

"Hey Doc, can I have more of these?
This Kid in my Tummy feels more
Horny than his Dad."

"Man, I hate how he loves using us as Bait,
Beverage and Beguilement!!!"

One thing about being a Public Spectacle above is you'd always have a Hungry Audience waiting down below.

"Great!! Thanks Genius for choosing to race near a PET STORE of all places!!!"

Always insist on a FULL Kiss from your Princess.

"Happy Mother's Day, Mum!"

It was instant silence again as the
Neighbors from Hell returned home.

Nothing beats getting stuck in
a Jam all morning with the Kids
when your Hubby calls.

Puberty was an extremely Mathematically Confusing time for young teenage Peter.

"Whoa. What's a Young Chick like you doing in a place like this?"

We soon realized that Flowers and Duct Tape wasn't nearly as smart as simply hiding amongst Flowers.

Who can resist Fresh Sushi? :)

"I'm serious Dave. Take the Stairs. These things gobble up everyone who goes in."

"Done fighting?"

"Mr Daniels, please be brave and answer the question:
do you feel Overworked?"

In the past, some Outposts were really, really hard to reach.

No Parking means No Parking no matter
where you're from.

"Oh! If you don't mind Doc,
I'd like to keep my Facemask on for today!
Viruses are everywhere!!"

"Hurry up."

Peter never expected the Radioactive Spider bite had Medical Complications down the road.

"It's tough kiddo. Everyone here is Hard-Pressed by these monsters who just push and push and push till they squeeze every Last Drop outta us."

Our Mum made it absolutely safe for us to cross the Road.

As a Raven, Ivan never imagined a new Heavenly Haven at the Tavern.

Bob made himself the most feared
Bird ever in the Himalayas with
his Flag-Collecting Hobby.

Working from home was really enjoyable –
just pretend to type on the keyboard whilst
your Spouse does ALL the Housework!

Tomato Funerals

"I dunno about you bro. I still feel Lost."

"Careful! That's Miss Direction.
The direction of her Direction
is always mis-directing."

Forbidden Fruit

"Car Killer? Is that the face of a Car Killer?
Car Crasher maybe. But hey -
most survive, right??"

Nothing beats Conscientiousness in the right Direction.

"NOOO!!!! ....mom, ...you...you....
can't compare Apples with Oranges!!!!"

Going to Dark Night Spots where no one can spot you can be a Tough Spot to be in.

Why good Fruit Punch always runs out.

"Go with him? Hmph! We won't get anything back from him after he gets voted in!!"

"Sure...Honey.....I'll do the laundry right after......I.....finish.....this...No....wait..."

The Trojan King's Shopping Addiction eventually doomed all the Trojans.

Some Books are worth Dying for.

"Dear Chris: where were you?
We waited and waited for your
Bladder and finally decided...."

"Hey kids, the hole in the wall's yours.
We're going with the Rat's nest of
a messy Sock Drawer here."

Getting your Kids to eat their Vegetables can sometimes
take Superheroic Help and Effort!!

"Well, you can't deny it. That fella's REALLY Subtle
about his Wife-hiding Camouflage."

What the Thinker has been thinking
of for a long, long time.

"I don't get it Laura. I thought
we fed the Zebras well. How did
they all die from Starvation??"

Ambitions can kill.

Mr Bond was left shaken by the price
of his Stir-Dried Laundry.

Ever the prankster, Posterior Specialist
Dr. Peters sneaks in a drop of Hydrochloric
Acid to test his patient's rear-end reflexes.

Jenny really hated her Hot Young Sardine
Boyfriend who ran off after her Pregnancy.

Scary Modern Fairly Tales

It was a Whole New World for Princess Jasmine once she had the Lamp.

Alice realised early on that it was far simpler
to just sit & relax, not stand around all day...

Unbeknownst to most Bible Scholars, the Ark was
History's first case of mass Sea Pollution.

"Yeah. All I HAD for Christmas were
my 2 Front Teeth, my 2 Front Teeth, YES!
My 2 Front Teeth!! ....that's why I wanna
kill all Dentists out there!!"

"Can't shake it off, Officer Jenkins!!
This gut feeling the Murder Victim's
Body's right here!!"

Vomit Poetry

How the first Flag in human history
was invented.

Daddy Duties can be Murderous.

It's horrendous being stuck between
a Giant Donut & a Mountain of Donuts.

"You Idiots!!! I said worship Me!!
Not WARSHIP Me!!!!"

It helps to paint your Drone female and sexy
when you study horny male Bumblebees.

The Painful Reality for your Weekend after Friday Night.

Sabertooths would be a delight for today's Modern Dental professionals.

Romantic Advice from Amoebic Parents can be REALLY Shocking.

"We heard you couldn't sleep."

"Well, dead or alive, Genius is in
Hot Soup now."

Retail Origins

How Julius Caesar taught his Baby
Messenger Birds to fly.

Legal Thinking

Smaller Fish Bowl residents do love Larger,
more tempting Fish Food bottles.

For painfully obvious reasons, Tarzan didn't remain
Lord of the Apes for long after his new Travel Habit.

"……you don't suppose we're next on the Menu, right?"

Parental Lessons can get confusing with Armadillo dads who are Basketball fans.

Jim's limbs were deemed too trim by his Dream Gym.

As their Love decayed, Richard and his Wife started living in separate Nests in the same Home.

"You mean the World to me Honey…!! Just let me head off quickly before I head off quickly to meet you, okay?"

In their race to the top, only one of the Dogs realized how having Penthouse Access was the Key to Success.

How 2 Crocs came up with a Global Footwear empire.

Nurses with degrees in Nursing and
Literature can be really Stressful.

"Don't mind him if he confuses you.
He's not really good with Verbal Recall."

Rex Jr's new Brick Hobby was soon Extinct in the
Rex Household after all the pain it caused.

"O Father, bless this Food that we receive before us with Thanksgiving....!"

Teachers on Cloud Nine.

Being stuck on a Deserted Island
makes no sense when you have
a huge Wooden Plank next to you.

Legal Comedians

It really hurts to find out you're the Adopted one in the Nest when a Fire breaks out and your brothers fly off.

Never Date a Snake at a Swamp.

Nothing's worse than running out of Toilet Papyrus as your Papyrus Tiger looks on.

"Careful! YOU might get lost in the crowd here!!"

Lois stared in the direction of her Super Villainous Husband who loved Flying off during Domestic Tiffs he couldn't win.

One logistical advantage of being a Tortoise Parent is you can have Peace and Quiet immediately.

With the help of the Polar Bears community the Home Quarantine program of the North Pole was the most effective in the whole World.

Never dump the Pied Piper after
your First Date with him.

"For crying out loud Jenny, will you stop
photo-Instagraming every Half-eaten
thing we eat?!"

It's hazardous to work as a Cleaner at the Dinosaur Museum – your Supervisor can make you Extinct.

"But Sir, Sir!! SHE made me do it!!!"

Inheritance Woes

Queen Beatrice decided enough was enough and got Social Distancing away from ALL of her noisy children!

It is unwise to go Bananas for lunch before you go Bananas for your Date.

It's great being Dressed to Kill when eating out.

Gerald forgets that staying in his Home and
wearing a Facemask doesn't help his Bowels.

How to spot a Future Lawyer.

Joey's dietary needs as a Giant Vulture were easily met by Fresh Food which came to him.

The First Marriage Proposal in Human History came from a misunderstanding Mary had with William.

Surviving a Plane Crash can sometimes depend on the Strength of your Trousers.

Eve learns what's Good and Bad and chooses accordingly.

Most Historians had no idea that the 3rd World War was actually started by a Cleaning Lady in Washington.

Early Speech

We were lucky the Ant-eater who often terrorised us loved Chocolate Bars and one was near our Nest!

"You little idiots!! Does it look like WE need Facemasks for that silly Virus thingy?!!"

"Careful. Mum feeds that evil Robot our Underwear."

Never offend other Sushi Chefs responsible for buying Eels in the morning.

The Ostriches' Celtic holiday got really confusing when they visited Scotland.

"Whoa Joe. Something tells me you better cool it on all that Sneezing."

Giraffes make the worst Divers.

"Honey, seriously think you're Overweight."

Unbeknownst to most, Ali Baba was a Shrewd Greedy Boss who once had 400 Thieves.

The Mental urge to jump in and eat them
was somehow really unbearable at times.

No need to be Humble. Sometimes it does
help that you look like a Star!

"Why, how did you guess?? I DO have a few
Screws loose…!!!"

"Errrr….. esteemed Leader,
I seriously don't think these
Earthlings want us as Conquerors."

It wasn't easy when Mary had a Little Lamb whose Fleece was as Wide as a Snowfield.

Never trust Property Agents who give Maps to your new home instead of a property deed.

"....Hey, look on the bright side!
Now you have something to explore
the Local Scenery with!"

Chris hated his mum for his new Smartphone which felt more like a Family Outing Leash.

To their dietary joy, the three Bears found Goldilocks went well with their Porridge.

My Mum paid the price for being too Nutty for Nuts in her younger Days.

A practical Joke at the Laboratory quickly went south.

"…..I'm afraid the Mountain of Evidence just hasn't HELD UP in Court today, your Honor!!"

"Give up!! You are Surrounded!!!"

"Sir, I think I'd hold all morning appointments. I believe you forgot to walk the Dog today."

A quick trip to the nearby Car Park gave the Ants their best Housing Renovation ever.

Never take family photos too slowly on
beaches with Photo-bombing Walruses.

Nobody liked looking up to
those Gangster Giraffes.

"Still don't get why they call this
Lambs to Slaughter Valley!!"

Marine geology takes you Everywhere.

It gets awkward when you realise the
Bank you're robbing isn't Financial.

The price of Privacy can
be a Painfully High one.

"Nothing's more Scary when one's Dentist
also handles your Home Discipline."

On slow afternoons, library staff often
felt the full brunt of Renowned
Writer Mr Harold's Writer's Block.

Nothing's more Stressful than
Celtic Mouse Traps.

Why Scottish Farms near the coast have the World's most quiet Chickens.

Celestial Technicalities can make Eternity unbearable.

Due to Technical Issues, Judy lost her Singing Competition by a staggering nine points.

Gravitational Misunderstandings

"Okay, you gutless Amphibians ......
your Snake's gone!!"

Must Study!

"Darn! Stop the Line! Stop the Line! ....those Love 'Boids are at it again!!"

"What do you mean the Map's confusing?? Use your Eyes ....it's just right there...!!"

"....have to admit! Being Solar-powered
makes me feel less guilty
about Deforestation!!"

"Polar Bear Lunches were never the same
again after the Internet was introduced.

Always keep a Salt & Battery far, far apart.

"Don't talk too loudly or they'd know
we're Tourists."

"Wow, really love these Celtic Highlands!!
Great view and Fresh Food falls from
the Sky!"

Some Knights in shining armor are
Natural Entrepreneurs.

Customers of the Panda Delivery Service never knew
why their Food always arrived half-eaten.

About the Author/ Illustrator

Jashorn (aka Jason Lee) received his BA in Psychology from the National University of Singapore. Born in Singapore, Jashorn often haunted Yamaha Music Shops during his misspent youth as a French Horn player. Jashorn is notorious among his friends for making them constantly smile and for organizing his Lego Minifigures by Marvel films. When not writing, Jashorn enjoys exploring the Internet, and prefers to support his other hobbies of reading and drinking too much coffee.